IN LABAN'S FIELD
Selected Poems

Norm Sibum

In Laban's Field

CARCANET

First published in 1993 by
Carcanet Press Limited
208-212 Corn Exchange Buildings
Manchester M4 3BQ

A CIP catalogue record for this book
is available from the British Library.
ISBN 1 85754 038 7

The publisher acknowledges financial assistance
from the Arts Council of Great Britain

Set in 11pt Galliard by Bryan Williamson, Frome, Somerset
Printed and bound in England by SRP Ltd, Exeter

Contents

The Seduction of Joseph

Some of you probably know the story –
how Joseph lorded it over his brothers,
snitching on them to their father, outdreaming
their dreams. He couldn't let it rest there,
and as sensitive as his mother
he stole his father's love.
Jealous, the brothers sold him, one night, into Egypt.
Joseph knew that he loved them, too.
Either he was dumb, or he was remarkable,
saying, 'It's not time, yet, to change these things.'
Only the fiercely proud or opportunists
can afford such outlooks.
There he was, bagged and lashed to a camel,
sailing the starlit desert,
beginning to grow up in order to grieve.
Like any poet worth his salt, he knew the future –
that time had given him a routine,
that he would softshoe his way into the pharaoh's court
and turn back the night
and steal the love of the pharaoh's people.
Who says that a life of glitter can't be lived
as one of high moral purpose and grace?

Joseph found work.
He found approval in his master's eyes.
And time unfolds, but never smoothly.
It's written in Genesis as a red-letter day:
the wife to Potiphar – one of the pharaoh's captains –
waylaid Joseph in her living-room,
adroitly parting his clean white garment.
With curling lips, with fanatic tenderness,
she got her eyeful, and Joseph blushed.
To tell it otherwise, I'd just get sentimental
and recount more of their idyllic childhoods.
I'd say she was a warm, high-spirited woman
to whom the future had been only partially revealed

1

or she wouldn't have made her move so playfully.
Clapping her hand to Joseph's genitals,
she reached for too much too fast,
and put the squeeze on all his fathers,
on his hopes for a future in the royal house.
Some of us have been there in the way that we bungle
our chance meetings, and stretch our loyalties.

And it's written that Joseph turned and ran,
left the woman with only that robe of his,
one that was embroidered with a pattern of stars.
And her longing and his attempt to think
were compromised by warranties outmoded even then,
calling for trust and more of the unpredictable.
Joseph cringed in some alley, his pride smarting.
The nameless woman recovered her equilibrium.
Let's imagine how lovers embarrass themselves
with kisses that explode or fructify empires
but permit business, art and politics to remain intact.
Maybe this is what we mean when we say someone
leads a secret life – some Fast Eddy of Desire.
The world you and I inhabit is new and random
even if it seems to be roasting over a spit,
but the sun, the moon and eleven genuflecting stars
comprised Joseph's favourite dream wherein
he was touched by grief and he wept.

By now it's obvious I'm looking backwards
through a realm of shadowy, dancing figures –
myself, a one-step dancer in a two-step routine.
And it won't be easy for some of you to convince me
that lovers don't play for keeps.
I'm no would-be hunter looking for grace
nor a simple farmer who wields a stick
in the shadows of downtown office towers
so that the sheaves of corn will fall
to the left and the right of my hard labour,
beating a path for the dancing universe
or for a king's ledgers and the magic of numbers.

But Joseph's story is as old as all that:
how he made adversity go to work for him.
And truly, I inhabit thought's backwaters:
something other than marginalia
marching like pinwheels into post-everything.
Somehow, I expect to take on the world
even when imagination and the itch for love
highlight my notebook like a tired soldier's
fallen arches. Guffaws, not fireworks,
herald the breakdown of our social contracts.

And though Joseph's story did end happily,
long he lived as the pharaoh's right-hand man,
he still had to do his time in a lonely cell.
His lovely seducer, seizing yet another moment,
reported his unseemly behaviour to her husband.
The butt of jailhouse jokes, Joseph languished.
Not guilt but boredom crowded his stolen kisses.
You know how it is with lovers: always, they fear
that they have just been kidding themselves.
And his fathers slept in his flesh by day,
and they turned up their noses by night
at the affection and the grain he dreamed
he would one day lovingly offer them.
Sometimes, as the torturous hours passed by,
he tried to recall the woman's face.
He may have known the future, but her features
remained elusive, and he tasted again the kiss
that did or didn't agree with him, but nonetheless
worked its own kind of change against the encroaching famine
in the land. Maybe this is what we mean
when we say that a kiss is bitter-sweet and time
stands still.

Only last night I saw Potiphar's wife again.
In a feature film shot cheaply in Cairo –
the woman, a studio girl kept around for bad actors –
juiced up the romance that exists between
the pyramids and America's freeze-dried products.

3

Could be just another barren fantasy
that a poet sleeping in northern latitudes might have.
On a dare, I'd kiss the playful woman.
I'd ignore recent revolutions or new wrinkles in thought,
so that when lions roar I'd know they're only hungry
and when people weep I'd know they've tasted justice.
Maybe I'm the latest clever dupe
to bring on yet another round of pain.
But unlike Joseph rising to a crisis,
managing it so that everyone could eat,
we, who need our future in order to milk our past,
surrender our moments to our torments
and extort profits, condemned to provide for no-one.

Abraham

Late in the day, a day too far gone
to counter with sudden urges or well laid plans,
I read how Abraham wandered from valley to valley
with his goods. I had figured him for a desert rat,
a collector of invectives no-one needs,
but he was only looking for a place to pitch his tent
and pasture his cattle, to live well.

It's like that now – journeys that become
an impulse to laugh along with the stars at our fortunes.
In the cabaret below me,
someone warms up an accordion.
And if that music won't break my heart
the loner seated there as always
stretches out his carafe of wine, anticipating
what fun the place will provide
after the waiter draws the curtain on the kisses
and the payoffs. And while the people below
do their last-minute shopping – their breath whitening
in the cold – I come away from watching them
absurdly thoughtful. Oblivious to consequences,
I will flog among the living what interests them least.

The first stars of the evening move into position,
advance scouts on routine manoeuvres.
The downtown lights take the horizon over,
glowing with the city's poisonous exhalations like ruins
in the distance. Now an old beggar rants at everyone,
and by our less imposing heaps of concrete and brick,
he curses his luck and thrusts his cane up at the abyss.
Every day his magic outdoes mine –
that he doubles over with a coughing fit
and brings forth his blind appetites, that he recovers,
and, purple-faced, shouts that Abraham was an outcast like him.

It is how the sky turns, how I am turning.
Beamed up from a warehouse parking-lot,
a pair of searchlights pierce the old body of love
with news of yet another bonanza – a carpet sale.
This firmament calls me to Abraham's knife and fire.
He found a place, and it kept him well.
But theatre overtakes him as he grabs
Isaac's throat – the fire consummating their mutual anguish.
The incoherent promises of the God go to seed,
and miracles take root in the world.
I keep turning the pages. The ambitious God caresses
the fertile cornlands, the blood-red stone of Edom.

With an impulse stripped of history,
all of us are trying to hang on –
if only to order or to disorder, to love's inflated
value. The edges of those possible affections
have grown blunted and more cruel.
Maybe Abraham was just another luckless poet
who began to regard the stars beyond the city as promises:
Those pleasant fields in Canaan, the God who said,
'Just go, and I will torment you with my experimental blessings.'
Like a poet of this century, the old beggar shuffles off.
Reeking in his overcoat, he lacks only an audience and a bottle.
And he will get no nearer to his sky than this:
a couple, kissing at the corner, draw the stars closer.
It is to say that nothing will change the monotony for them –
the swirling eternities of desire and death.

The Cave

You suffer from the usual afflictions of the spirit, my love.
How well you've known apathy, fantasy, remorse.
How quickly the years passed – everyday experience
acquitting you of the crime of age.
It was touch and go, but at last you finished the painting.
Now there's money in your purse – nice, crisp fifties,
and that's a better feeling, isn't it, than to leave your life
to lie exposed over a sink of dirty dishes?

And the celebration, such as it was, came off pleasantly
          enough –
even if our guest stayed longer than is his rule.
He was eager to rectify our ignorance of failure.
All winter you had paraded before me the angels
that you swiped from artbooks
and then put into flaming, outlandish disguises,
hoping against hope that no-one would object
to their rough-and-ready characters.
But when our dinner companion turned polite on you,
overcome by your crudely stated uncertainties,
you remained girlish, rational, unimpressed with yourself.
'Consolations,' our tipsy friend then tried to tell us,
'are dark events that we confuse
with god-sent solutions to our problems.'
Even the pompous must believe they, too, face facts.

And all winter you slept as deeply as a battered wrestler,
so much so your painting must be considered a miracle –
you, a female Jacob sporting tinted hair and sneakers.
To get the shape of an angel's hand was a true but considerable
task. There were no short-cuts. There were many questions:
Should an angel about town flash its garters?
Should it demonstrate among those lost a perfect ego?
Should the sky it flies out of be as blue as heaven can be?
You didn't know. And I still don't know for sure,
but closing on secret dossiers while you slept

your eyes previewed the crimes you will eventually commit
once you put the proportions of love down right.

And in this world of oversimplified virtue
I thought such virtuosity as yours a goner:
the angel's puckered mouth you drew
and the sailor that was dreaming the implications of it.
Your mother, who figured you wouldn't amount to much,
could only say – as she appraised your work –
'No angel wears lipstick, dear, but it's nice to see your looks
improved.' We may sustain direct hits and never recover.
Remember, though, that our injuries never close,
staying in business to collect such fresh insults
and fair weather as they can.

Anyway, you go ahead and have your bath. As you've said,
'The bosses don't want us to do anything but amuse
ourselves.' Accordingly, we've lived together.
But with spring's first flower I'll make yet one more pact.
Kneeling, I'll cup my hands to my imaginary plot of earth
while you cast the sky in vivid shades of pink again.
And, side by side in bed, still glowing from wine and want,
we can argue if sleep just consummates the same old kingdoms.
Or, more stealthy than dancing thieves in a dream,
we can bury the world for a few hours.

Maybe you will paint the sky blue for once.
Maybe an uprooted daffodil will break past
the heavily guarded borders of totalitarian streets,
rescuing the lost, bringing the guilty to justice.
But, most likely, I'll just spend tomorrow
delivering another kick at the old tin can of childhood.
For now, I'll phone our dearly departed guest.
I'll see if he got through the roadblocks
with his ideas of what is possible and what always remains
a write-off. Just like Plato said it was,
the universe is an enormous cave. How embarrassing
to get arrested in that immensity for drunk driving.

8

The Child

Beneath the grey sky the maples turn colour.
Leaves yellow or fade to a dull rust.
Sweet odours of fruit, ripening in the bins by the grocery-store,
mingle with the chill of approaching winter,
and I rely on their intransigence too much,
criss-crossed as this city is with its bleak avenues.
The shoppers grab handfuls of autumn.
They sort peaches or send them tumbling
in the twilight that wanders through our moods
and the chatter that sometimes sticks in our throats.
Lately, I've been dreaming that I chase a child
who's still small enough to jump into my arms.
But dreams are nothing unless they come out of the blue.
How can they compare to those tough Blue Damson plums?

So, count it a good day or a minor miracle
when uncontested longing isolates its object
in the realm of love's pure guesswork.
Each smile that threads a needle in this store
occupies gloomy Cinderellas of either sex
or belies the frank stares of old women.
Longing and death – those old Vita Nuova fantasies –
are one and the same computerized lottery.
Standing in line to buy cigarettes,
watching the cashier's fingers dance over the keys,
I overhear one woman say to another,
'Oh, Harry was heavy into the sauce.
Then his wife decided to move into town.
You see, in time, everything falls into place.'
The child has been saying in my dream,
'Let's play. I may be gone tomorrow,
or I may grow up into something you will despise.'

I will not name this child – it just wouldn't do.
I knew his mother. Probably, I loved her,
and what does that mean but that her name

has always conjured up for me the harvests and the first
ground frosts – the mistaken expectations and dreams?
I could ramble on this way forever,
inflating the worn-out broken heart of our times,
waxing as nostalgic as radio personalities
who turn time around with songs about cars
in which lovers speed off into the sunset –
Plato's dialogues stashed like six-packs in the trunk.
Cervantes wrote about protracted loneliness.
He was poor and a failure but, smelling pay dirt,
he tacked on more and more episodes as the autumns
came and went – all this just to deal bucolic sensitivity
its death-blow! All this just to buy cigarettes!

Seeing those faces bent so close to the fruit,
eyes full of daydreams and unlucky pasts,
don't blame me if my mood yields
to drunken stupors, arthritic aches, withdrawal panic.
The cashier curls her toes, watching the clock –
her time advancing in little stutter steps,
and though I might guess at what she waits for,
it's clear she would rather be elsewhere.
No cop comes around to shake down the wind
for prowling about the beans that dry in their bins
or for molesting passersby outside – or the maples.
But, plunging through a crowd at the door,
an old woman with a crumpled bag of apples
shuts me up before I can put this question to her:
'On what terms do you fight the great struggle?'
This is the withering heat of her answer:
'Not by anything you know, Sonny Boy!'

Later on, in my room, I close my eyes,
and along with my dream of the child,
I attempt to send sleep back into its own territory.
I can no more account for the fact
that the kid isn't mine to play with
than I can for the cost of Chinese greens –
even if the prices are more reasonable here than elsewhere.

'Answers aren't everything,' I tell myself.
If his grandparents were spoilers and lushes,
if his mother was crazy about the scent of wet alder
and the smell of bread frying in bacon grease,
if she touched herself like a Venus while dreaming
with sleepwalking, frightened, grasping fingers,
replacing what the world took from her body,
this child's lot could have been worse than it is.
He has her bone structure, her shape of hand.

The pearl-grey streaks of cloud darken, and below,
the grocers haul in the produce for the night.
Parked by the curb, biding his time,
a T-shirted adolescent races the engine of a gleaming Camaro
while the cashier cashes out inside the store.
As I've already said, she, too, is waiting,
but any moment – at that instant when she grabs her purse
and steps quickly toward the car's shelter –
the crude, uneasy realignments with space,
the ice age, will render her breathless.
And from each cloud Pythagoras leers at us.
I light the cigarette it took me so long to purchase,
and for one last time the child laughs in my dream.
His face glows with health, with brittle affection.
Maybe I could have told him something
about the One and the Many, about two plus two,
or about the light we generate like sweat.
It is an unequal contest between mercenary wills.
In the dream he soundly defeats me,
and by daylight I send him on his way.
And in neither realm do we touch.

Portoferraio

Outside the albergo,
the birds were as restless as the air.
An old woman screeched in the piazza.
She had a bird's nest for hair.
Through the tall and wide windows –
the double shutters thrown back –
there was view enough of a world,
and guests checked-in from distant parts.
But the bells and the distant thunder,
maids chattering up and down the halls,
were like storybooks to my ears –
momentous but unremembered tales.

The commonplace was just that:
events hadn't passed from life there.
It said something for faith –
should one have lost the power of the idea.
But the words of that woman
getting such volume out of her lungs,
were incomprehensible to me.
I took in the windowbox of geraniums,
the cistern below no-one used,
or would take seriously again –
save dogs marking their territories.
She, just waking, possessed the room with her eyes.
She, sitting up, came to her whereabouts, surprised.
She asked, 'Isn't this nice?', and I answered, 'Yes.'

How familiar it seemed!
And add to the voice that was bringing
god knows what to us, I heard another:
mine saying 'Hello' to the storm on the sea
still dim in its power – love no crueller than a fable now,
a game the kids had put to song,
skipping rope, coaxing Time out into the open.

Let me say the bed dwarfed us.
It mocked infancy and middle-age,
and if it turned a profit, it had its character.
One gets starved, sometimes,
for the birds that suddenly flood the air
and just as suddenly disappear...

The boughs lifted, dropped, and swayed.
So many leaves, disturbed, rode the wind –
the grey-black sky heaving on its side.
I was proud of her, proud of me –
our room and its walls irrelevant now
to any argument but the tempest gathering.
Secure in our cave of limbs,
we parted lips, maintained form,
while the kids below, at the last instant,
grabbed their ropes and deserted the square.
They shouted 'It's going to rain!', laughing and triumphant.

Then, thunder rifled across the sky.
And deep in the body, from their separate places,
old prayers met and whined, and rose up – a brute force.
Clouds broke open. Rain pelted windows.
Rain plastered leaves, poured over stones,
sought every opening, every fissure,
and Time was washed – love and hate submerged.
Beaten down, the flowers sprang back bright as ever.

It was a kind of incarceration – that spell,
heaven: to have no thought for anything,
to slide like raindrops down the glass,
colliding and mingling. Such transparent intentions!
Then, thunder rumbled at the other end of the world.
The old woman returned and screeched.
Birds flew, or sat and ruffled feathers.
The kids brought out the ropes again,
sang, and danced on the storm's grave.

Jeremiah

It's tricky shouting the old prophet down,
each word of mine a hired dancer.
Each tear Jeremiah dejectedly squeezes
for the lewdly trashed body of his bride
seems like stale news of overrated crime.
Late now, there is still homage to be paid
to the wind that blows and the sky that clears
and to the swaying of the trees –
where, below, the street-cleaner checks his watch
and drags his shovel along the curb.
Our yearned-for heartland doesn't exist,
and the stars announce that winter is standing by.

And each leaf that hangs suspended in darkness
hardens along with the passionate extremes
of human kingdoms, a prophet's stubborn moods.
In order to loosen things a little,
I sidle up to the nearest body, and with dry chatter
I unleash my thoughts and spread my troubles.
I count life's highlights on one hand –
the whining child's unslaked thirst,
old age's yellowing dance of canes.
Everything that leaks out of gaseous wells
is a matter of unhumble opinion.
In other words, I could make my way down
to the bottom of some prophet's broken cistern
and blend into the pattern of things there.

Otherwise, stuff my body full of straw
and plant it in the nearest cornfield –
away from those kids tossing firecrackers below,
wailing like cop-cars, doing wheelies with their bikes.
Their primordial impulses are going high-tech,
and someone should revoke their licence to operate, too.
The cabaret begins to shut down,
and lovers on their sleazy dates leave a good time –

noses prickling from the odours
of ionized curses and overheated brake linings.
The women scuffle by in high heels
and the men expectantly jangle car-keys.
The self they defend by their dreams
has been an expensive proposition to maintain.

Soon, the city will sleep like a winded beast,
and somewhere, a fledgling prophet might find
honest people breaking their hearts for wages.
There is no guarantee,
and, with a lump rising in his throat,
he'll feel he has grovelled long enough,
scouring every inch of sour property the world has,
only to end up drowning in what
delinquent gods spit between clenched teeth.
He will wish to renew negotiations with those
who manage the conditions for prophecy.
I'm much better off than Jeremiah was –
at least I can carry a change of clothes
for the cold, wet, heartless nights.

No poet can honour or move the earth,
lamenting that the bride and groom of love
have broken up. Yet, stupidly, I work,
thinking to rebuild the City of Heaven overnight,
to populate it with my dearest friends,
to fill their empty jars with cheap wine.
While those trees below spin around in the wind,
women impatiently swing their purses
and men still fumble with their car-keys.
Only yesterday, I compared the self
to the kind of second thoughts I get
when I, too, return to objects of my desire
some compliment – every little move I make
is an adventure in free-form diplomacy, in righteousness.

So, like an old sailor, I lie on my back
and stare at the ceiling. And sometimes,
I forget just where this cheap room is –
LA, Thebes or some other valley
about to be deprived of its native splendour
by hard-heartedness, profiteers, false dreamers.
Men still prize their habitats and pleasures.
They still sleep in postures
of humiliation, dread and thwarted lust.
And the effort to get something right
still mixes in my mouth with the god's breath –
as Jeremiah's did, as Jeremiah tasted it.
And that is enough to cause most people to lose
their breakfasts, despising again
the worn-out materials, the everlasting doom.

But when the lovers on the street stop necking,
then buckle up and cruise away,
it becomes easier to remember where I am.
I imagine the sound of rustling nylons,
of lighters being flicked, of the voices Jeremiah heard
from the wells he was flung into
as punishment for his pride and gloom.
The lovers yawn, young enough to remain awake
and add loneliness to their images
of the land and the self, and of precious substances.
Ragged and yellow, the leaves talk, too –
those weeping countenances drooping from branches,
infested with parasites and the burden of desire.
Now and then, one breaks free and drifts down.

Hibs and Lil

The moon? It is a thing in the sky,
sometimes, rushing to meet its star:
furnace shanked above loneliness,
heat a law or a prejudice put there.

Winter? It has come to rescue Lil
with a remembrance of her childhood,
cold fishingtowns and loggingcamps
a concern for origins draws closer.

She might step outside the apartment now,
beneath the metropolitan heaven:
the moon and star – pristine smudges
that are empowered to humble her –

and she might forget what people said
about their lives an hour ago
when men and women laughed and cared,
and then waved goodby to Hibs and Lil.

*

Death? It is only a word in art,
and all Hibs need do is lie down by Lil,
and refrain from talking lack of worth
as it only makes for surplus-value.

But then, even Lil has slept with losers,
and even now, expects greatness.
To shunt death aside for the duration...
the qualities required might shatter Hibs.

'What deceptions the old ones practised,
nothing so denatured as our consciences –
that, through the oesophagi of large birds,
from the other side of wall or ceiling,

charlatans of health cleared their throats
and spoke curatives to the sick,
and it was not so much an idea
as a preoccupation with playfulness.'

Guests who had attended the party
to argue any matter, agreed with Hibs
that Burckhardt, the source of the tale,
stretching up his neck to art and God,

still kept aloof from the effects,
and gave all the more to science.
For there is no innocence when one has a life.
In young cities, there's even less.

*

Death is only a word in art,
and all Hibs need do is say, 'Dear,
I told you it would be like this.

That when guests argue Tibet and China,
and when that Mr Venus suggests
how new microbes from outer space

ought to engender enough new forms
that we can kiss goodbye the housework,
well, it is only so much more politics.'

But Hibs said nothing, and out Lil went
for a breath of the winter air,
and glancing at the cold bits of dawn,

nowhere to go, perceived her extinction:
there would be no more remembering
her childhood in the Edgewater Hotel.

Once, it had floats for her father's plane,
and once, it had happier drunks,
and the music? One could hear it,

hear the song 'Your Cheatin Heart'
spill out of the place like whisky
from the shacks that rimmed the bay.

*

This is how it gets, sometimes –
these chill mornings on the coast:
the pale moon and one pale star
closing the gap at the end of graveyard shifts.
But then, empty-handed, free to fail,
strong enough still to cross over the range
of her hips and on – to her face and kiss,
Hibs, wanting insurance, chased Lil the oracle.

And she contended that she was fine,
and turned from him to her other side
with her dress and secret pleasures,
and when she yawned and said, 'That moon?',
Hibs responding, surprised them both:
it is but a thing in the sky,
cold with our nightmares, cold with its rock,
that, sometimes, rushing to meet its star,
leads the way to a last embrace.'

In Laban's Field

Like Jacob, who wrestled an angel in his sleep,
like 4½ billion of our earthly companions,
you and I strain after paradise and cheat a lot,
favouring our hips, mimicking some timeless truth.
I could be greeting the end of the world.
I could be looking at you from a great distance,
absent-mindedly stroking your face
while, gently, we give in, hang out or die
on our portion of this used-up earth.
Even worse calamities could befall us.
For openers, we're losing our youthful looks.

It is mid-afternoon, the end of winter,
and so far, as we outlast it and lie down together,
it's clear we've been too melancholy
to squander what remains on thoughts of virtue.
Whenever we dream of old men with long beards,
of young women waiting for handsome strangers,
like Sunday-school kids we get to know
the crime-ridden book of Genesis.
Like all meek and intelligent people,
we shy away from the outspokenly virtuous
who wrestle too many angels in public.
And because all gestures emanate from dull senses,
from half-remembered stories,
and from our half-articulate talk,
as a token of your esteem for me
you draw me even tighter to yourself.

Imagine that the sun is low in the sky.
Imagine that the day has been sweltering –
that the young man, Jacob, a thief, walks out of the hills
and comes upon Laban's prosperous fields.
A lovely woman stands at the well.
Imagine an unlikely thought pops into his head:
he will talk about god with this Rachel,

showing off, ridding that well of the stone that blocks it.
He will even admit that the handful of water
with which he splashes his hot and dusty face
is no more than the sky's once-visible tears
and the earth is no more than the god's undoing.
You've often wondered what I think about
when I bury myself in your hair.
And always I answer it's not interesting –
the images smudged, the content tiresome,
that coming up short against one's mortality
is nothing an aspirin or a bullet couldn't cure.

Appropriately, we fall into that mood of Uccello's –
he, a dead painter, an early master of the line.
He knew how not to include too much,
but our craving for beauty sucks us into his paintings again.
As the limits of sanity shift
between the deadpan faces of knights on horseback
and art's necessary requirement,
we see men decked out in fatal finery,
engaging others who are aided by fear,
and caught in battle, all quest after death's great silence.
I can't say why this painting moved me.
I was bored and restless that day in the gallery.
Most likely, I will never know, and now we kiss,
and we still embrace what perspectives we can.

Then there is an attitude peculiar to Mohammed:
when painters paint they sin against God.
Come the general hilarity of Judgment Day,
angels will bid them breathe life into their works
or persuade them to recant their gilded mistakes
as though paradise will be content with flowers
that one can smell, eat or hold up against Time.
It is on such waves of vengeance that paradise shadows us.
Imagine that Jacob begins to feel at home by the well,
juggling bad choices in his thoughts,
that as his eyes rest on the lovely Rachel,
he considers taking even more liberties with her dreams.

You may ask, as Rachel did,
'What has it to do with me?
A handful of water, a painting, a moment of fantasy
are sometimes the same gesture –
honest if mysterious wages paid to the spirit.'
I'll answer, 'No-one thinks like that these days,
and maybe it's for the best.
It's been a long time since Jacob in love,
a thief among thieves, stood speechless by the well.'

Imagine that he's not a complete stranger,
that he's only just come from Rebekah's side
to work in his uncle's fields.
Imagine him saying, 'It went off like a dream, like magic –
how Rebekah made me wear that goatskin coat
so I would smell as ripe and feel as hairy
an Esau to my blind father.
It was like a dream, I tell you,
how I stole what was my brother's –
his birthright in Isaac's great dream of plenty –
Isaac pawing at me, his breath reeking of wine,
his eyes watery with the notion that art is sinful.
Rebekah was both soft and hard.
And she said that my father was displeased with me,
that my brother has gone into the hills
to sing himself songs.
But it seems that Isaac's dream of eternity
and Rebekah's handicraft are working to my advantage.'

The liberties we take with each other
that increase the sensation we're in the pink
cause me to forget we are partners
in love without the benefits of eternity.
But you can see I've been thinking about Jacob,
about all who came before him and after,
about the moment he looked Rachel up and down by the well.
A past that weighed too much unfolds
and now opens to your weightless notions of love and chance,
to the tacky images of your lust,

to your aimless talks with the frothy universe –
as though, like Rachel, you choose
between a stranger's promises and those mistakes
you've always regretted making.

And if time keeps pounding at the hills,
whose secrets only Adam knows,
you advise me how much better it is to be happy.
It's another argument you win,
and I promise, once more, I'll lighten up.
But not even levity will reconcile
the differences we've incurred, experiencing virtue.
Our parents shouted out invitations
to join them in the farthest reaches of Genesis
until weary of that pounding in our ears
we doubt that there is evil.
Imagine that Rachel in Laban's tent
conceals beneath her skirt an image –
one she lightly fingered and adores –
and Laban, with a mutiny on his hands,
finding her out, respects that she's in the way
of women. It's all so confusing –
she and Jacob about to run off together
and live the monumental life,
contesting Laban's pride in his possessions.

Or, we pass on to some higher difficulty:
the time that Isaac blessed is treacherous –
that moment eternity always wants from us,
the ecstasy we can always provide
if only we could learn to keep our composure
and not increase each other's loneliness.
Maybe we need new models for our instruction,
for someone else to show us how to be amorous,
which is like saying Aphrodite still exists
or that there must be intelligent life on other planets.
Or we could outfit Jacob with a new prosthetic –
we could replace his wonky, angel-damaged hip
and charge it to the government.

Everything I've said may be too far-fetched
but for want of easier comforts of our own I don't care.

Laban gave to Jacob the most menial of tasks.
He strung him along year after year,
and still, Jacob kept in good humour
even after he was rewarded with his first wife, Leah,
even after he went into her and her handmaiden.
But all that time he wanted Rachel.
Nothing works the way it's advertised,
and because our hearts possess no more wisdom
than their mechanical replicas,
and because all systems have their mysterious glitches,
we envy lovers who bend, even break the rules.
Imagine now that many seasons have passed,
and Jacob, an upright toiler in Laban's fields,
has, as yet, no land to settle his household on.
Imagine that Leah is better than Rachel in the sack,
and imagine that by Jacob's larcenous sweat
he will sire an army and steal sweet Rachel from herself.
For he is cast between the angels and the beasts
and his hands weigh as much as overburdened books.

I know you have little trouble imagining all of it.
In your eyes I read it over and over again:
time does have a way of closing over fools –
there's no-one in this bed but us!
And this is the limit passion brings us to:
to know a thing explains either all or nothing.
And as the day comes around to night,
and as we must soon eat, we drag ourselves to the kitchen,
confessing we're always deepening our ignorance.
In Laban's field our moment, too,
would have been only briefly tender,
and now it seeps through a closing rift
in the ever-hardening scheme of things –
into legislation, tough-mindedness, indifference.
Someone in the far-off past arouses you, you tell me,
and above, the winter sky tips on end,

and darkness, and what remains of the sweet
heavy dust of painters swirls about us.
Through a similar fissure in the heavens,
Jacob thought he saw his angels.

We've eaten and done the dishes,
propelled by the drowsy force of habit.
Our eyes have grown misty from reading books.
We fall into bed again, this time to sleep.
And older than Adam and Eve, than memory,
the images in our dreams suggest
that vengeance is our only wage,
that we feed it to each other and swoon.
It hardly matters how, long ago, in Persian cities,
zealots shielding their eyes stripped the palaces of art,
piled the icons into heaps and torched them –
gold and silver torrents of god, angel and man
flooding the streets. Wrapped around you,
I laugh and cry – a flame of another kind.
We've been almost everywhere tonight – in Genesis,
and here, where mercy between men also knows no limit,
we dream the incontinent dreams of the lost.

Gardens of the Night

We climb, holding hands, to that grotto in Vancouver –
Jocelyn and I at large at this evening hour.
No empire dies just once,
and she's worn her nightmares of the end
as though they were party dresses.
And if the time of the year fails to coincide
with any festival known to us – no matter.
I say the word *earth*. I try to say it with affection,
disdaining that other word, *planet*.
It's too harsh a word for the garden we come to,
even if the garden could easily have become another
parking-lot. It's only by the mercurial agencies of art
that men and women will be led to believe
they are one with the objects they trash.
But, to hear them talking,
encumbered as they are with brochures and cameras,
they're more successful than I at naming
the zinnias, daisies, begonias and phlox.

Sing your praises! From here, in all directions,
the city stretches along maple-lined boulevards.
In nature, men are not born identical.
But in politics, provide them with a view
of a prosperous-looking city, of clean-looking water,
they'd half believe all men must be equal.
New properties scale the slopes to the north.
Pollution hovers over the refinery in the east.
In the west – the sun is the colour of a dirty apricot.
Southward, a phalanx of condos guards us from America.
Beyond that lie more suburbs and the border.
I say 'Forty miles hence is Old Country,'
and Jocelyn laughs, retouching her lips with lipstick.
Somehow, her bright intransigence is reassuring –
that I see in the shining of her dark eyes
how the lame walk, how the garrisons coarsely joke,
how drifters dream in the shade of cypresses.

Already she grabs my arm, wanting to leave.
But perversely, I enact the events of Gethsemane –
how an angel wipes the brow of Christ,
how Peter drunkenly sleeps a few paces removed
and so avoids placing his life in jeopardy,
how the evening is warm, the wine a soporific,
how Peter's loutishness could hardly pass for higher conduct.
Jamming my hands into my pockets,
I deny the reality of this revery three times
before the cock crows and interrupts for a moment
some long night of political terror –
the day breaking as if terror didn't exist.
Christ prays. The people keep whoring – that is,
they eat, drink, suffer and die,
and don't see how it should be otherwise.
And a few sentimental priests, addicted to power, know
they have this latest usurper dead to rights.
'Speak to me,' Jocelyn says, 'you're in a stupor again.'
Oh, she'll chat on about matters of spirit,
but usually throws her lot in with mental health.

Begin then with this most privileged of humanity.
No one of them may be so rich or pampered
that they needn't expend the energy to walk a little,
but neither with humble implements do they
scratch barren soil just to have being.
In fact, there's so much being on parade here
that I wonder where the world will have room for it all,
that, by mere use of one's eyes,
anyone can cultivate the Crucifixion.
Anyone can lay up treasures in their storage lockers
while stroking the unassuming flowers with dreamy voices.
Jocelyn didn't know which dress to wear for the occasion.
I had told her, 'It's only a garden.
The tourists will be crawling all over everything.'

At last, the angel departs and Christ goes to die,
and one might think that this should be the end of it –
me, throwing my voice across a few more rocks,

reticent even as I praise the flowers
and push Jocelyn in the direction of the parking-lot.
She rearranged the garden to suit her taste,
and, arguing that she still believes in Nature,
she accused me of witholding from her its bounty.
I could have picked her a bright bouquet
and answered her affection with ardent lips,
shielding her from the use I made of her eyes.
But here the flowers already ache from our caresses,
and no-one, betrayed, was ever satisfied with a kiss.

A Dispatch to Commodus

*After Marcus Aurelius died, Commodus with-
drew the army from the frontier, arguing that
Rome could not afford the expense, though he
went on to strap the treasury with extravaganzas
organized around himself.*

At the end, what changes?
Objects still carry the momentum,
This man dying – he's irrelevant,
this one whose soul disengages.
Cloth and bowl and campstool,
tentskin, brazier, charcoal –
these and a few personal effects
common to any ordered household –
stiffen and shut death out
from their autonomous preserves.
We, their living agents, grasp
what has weight and consequence,
and as we appraise how little we matter,
objects lend us justification –
even under a foreign sky,
even with wind and snow outside.
Snow dusts the camp,
yesterday's half-thawed earth,
and what's death to it?
Snow enslaves and softens contours,
muffles the silent forest,
then, melts away come Spring.

Now, this centurion brings fresh water.
'Yes, good. Put the jar there. Be off.
Get something warm in you, lest you catch your death.'
Irrelevant – that man in skins on a cot.

Irrelevant, yes, but Sleep reviews him.
And Necessity inspects the fever,
and thinning hair divides into comic shapes
a forehead looking for some relief.

Sleep reviews, Necessity inspects.
And the man's eyes, sinking like stones,
go back to kiss the brain and sue,
so as to get the kindest eulogy for a life,
once mastered, now ebbing away.

At the bugle's call, let the guards change over.
Let the tribesman in the forest guess
why a Roman should exchange
rude town for frontier outpost.
Caprice and delusion, as always –

crows with wings half-spooked –
find what they need to know,
picking at decayed import: Commodus in Vindobona!
Now terrifying his lovers in the taverns,
he who has no head, no heart,
will accept the Imperial Standard,
but will throw the game-plan out
and march away from exhaustion come Spring.

*

It is the dead hour.
A life hardens.
It approaches a precipice –
the mouth loose.
I dampen this once austere face
with a cloth soaked in water. I ease the vertigo –
all intention entranced by the embers of the fire.

*

Soon, men will prod others from a thick sleep.
They, beating the cold from their bones,
will draw close to the fires and curse the day
they left farm and wife. What's to tend here
but a phalanx, a latrine? What's to do but shovel –
the earth a paste of snow and lime and stench?
This man, however, he's done with these preoccupations.
He's done with mountains, seas, and forests,
with gerry-rigged potentates in deserts.
He's done with foul weather, foul food, foul men,
with painted enemies, with hangers-on
at our heels from camp to battle and back again,
and would have us invincible so long as it suits them.
But that I should praise, Marcus Aurelius,
the birds and the blossoms come Spring –
is this the only objective of your sickness?
'Commend Commodus to the gods,' you whisper,
'Send him to me so that I might bestow
a father's blessings on my son. He'll come around.'
No, not that heartless, heedless whelp,
who will forgo what rigors the gods demand,
and have it written he was equal to them.
Better that he stay in Vindobona and drink,
and let friends complete the corruption nature intended.
Better this than let the rot infect the earth.

*

Get on with your dying, Marcus Aurelius.
What can you be hanging on for?
I, for one, see it's over.
I am tired and bored,
and there's my house half-finished on a sunny coast,
a garden to put in and wine to ferment.
I, for one, will visit the mess,
drink something hot, shovel down some gruel.
When asked, 'How goes the patient?',

31

Citing your cares and the climate,
any old soldier's need for rest,
I'll keep your true condition from the officers –
all of them sniffing at the rumours,
and buy good men the time they need:
your precious Commodus a bad business,
your death indulging love and sealing our fates.
Even I must consider the future,
and what a picture it would make:
me – wrists opened – dead beside you.
But no, it's too much the old school.
I'll just play the one card I have,
I will tramp through snow and mud,
and from over there, at the ridge,
look out across the plains
at horizons that always seem fixed on a map,
where a few crows take flight,
bone-piles holding up the sky for them.
Then, I will praise Spring for you, Marcus –
your fields and your foolish colts,
and I will laugh at your soul – as per instructions.
After that – who knows?
Death by Commodus – here, or in Rome?

*

Now, old friend, I set right again
this bowl and this cloth rich with old tasks.
You upset them with your arm. A convulsion blew you apart,
and whether you spoke from rule or heart,
these, I think, may be deemed your last words:
'Say that if Hadrian built his cities,
I took care of emptiness and piled the dead bodies there.'
Good, it is finished – the soul gone off,
and the doctor cuts a figure no less absurd
than deactivated bone, nerve, sinew, and gristle,
and he will go and sleep with a woman,
and in her company drink himself blind drunk.
However, first things first: to Commodus a note.

'Greetings. It has been a long, tedious campaign.
It has been as meaningless in victory as in defeat.
Light snow falls here. Your father's no more,
dead this dawn after a fight with the unknown.
We await our direction. Come take your army,
                                        – Diotimus, physician.'

To Angie Skov

They are always vintage – these fountains,
especially in cities like this one
where a bell politely rings the hour
and the young and the old occupy benches.
From out of tales of death and corruption
that innocently fill the pages of dailies,
wrapped in scarves, in the boredom of precious light,
the huddled people greet events.

Here in the park, I invite myself home.
I mean it only as a figure of speech:
home is merely where one winds up,
the wind starting to push at the leaves –
the water in the pool now black.
My face reflected there – how embarrassing!
This is it? This image – my soul's house

that I pine for so as to integrate,
so as to withstand so many forces?
There are words to ponder over,
ones delivered in the tone of our mother's voice.
She, smiling, scowling, so knowing, girlish,
heavy on our roots, easy on the uprooting,
is unable to describe anything but her aches –
while alluding to a noble past.
Now, add themes and sentiments from various books
that you've been indulging, lately,
and we might arrive at a picture....

Words of princes, congresses, matinées,
of shots fired against a nation-state,
of Metternich, Talleyrand, Ciano, Chamberlain,
not to mention Rilke who walked this same garden,
and others who, devoted to the future,
now find the ambience historical....
Whether I claim or reject it, I just grab empty air –
always the moment, sick of that tyranny.

The wind, still pushing, drives the leaves around,
and your brother – kid with a dreamer's smile –
between the vaporous past and the vapours of better days,
hands in pockets, lounges by the pool,
admitted but unnoticed in this prim atmosphere.
Yes, the flowers resemble mother's vague nostalgia,
those marigolds spilling out of white urns,
while the shades of statues and heroes sleep –,
and she lies that she had once read poets.
Grandfather, for all time, dangles from a rope.
He casts his shadow all the way to America
from that tidy, suburban Berlin apartment.
1977, and each Willi Brandt saluting, 'Aufwiedersehn'.

To you, sister – only this: of healing there's none.
Whatever the material or progress
employed to disguise the slaughtered and maimed,
it's blind. Otherwise – now, cloudy in Paris.
A cold but not unpleasant light
pacifies the sleepy and the prosperous.
Mothers rock babies, lovers curl against lovers,
and the pigeons nestle on the arms of old men.
And I stand here remembering – the image now quiet –
how grandfather and I in some old castle town
gazed at the river's dragonflies,
my little fist buried in his.
Another bell, another hour, and soon, I'll send
this window, this dispatch of delights on its way.

Propertius in May

If you hate your life, you'll hate the people in it.
And remain indifferent to the antics of the state,
the barbarians who run things will bury you
with their cash-and-carry attitudes
toward the gentler celebrations of living.
Love yourself unduly and you'll play the sycophant
to everyone else's idyllic accounting of their careers.
But if you want to see justice done
you'd have to jail all citizens.

Myself, I'll never know what Propertius looked like.
Was he short, pugnacious? Was he tall and bland-talking?
Did he reach skyward for his thought
that hovered there for him like the moon,
eternally oppressive, ornamental, self-absolving?
I do know that sex and politics are a poet's lot.
Actually, they are everyone's headache.
The month is May, and it arrives hard on the heels
of a desire to quit this street, this city.

Rhododendrons, lilacs bloom everywhere.
It is the old arrogance of spring.
Even on Eastend pavement it casts its leafy shadows.
And despite my personal failures in romance,
social breakdowns always have their uses:
One can walk around feeling one goes one better
than the perpetrators of bad solutions.

My place may lie elsewhere as it always has,
on a bed some old lover is still paying off –
she, playing the bride awaiting her hero and his hormones,
extending her thin, brittle arms to the violence.
Once I fooled around with a woman like that.
Eventually, both of us chickened out,
because I detected in my heart's downtrodden thudding
repression, intolerance, sterility, complete philosophic systems.

In those days I lived my life
like it was a sentence that could go on for half a book,
one that she said she had read already.

But what does it matter, really?
Almost everyone finds delight
even in the most arid climates of affection.
Myself, I participate in the global rumour mills
that maintain the threat of the planet's imminent demise,
and I contribute to the local ones
tall tales of who's sleeping with whom.
I remember a night when the lover I courted
peered into the darkness of her bedroom
and maybe heard or saw or felt something:
A childhood event, an urgent call to behave better,
a searing pang of unrequited conscience.
She began to tremble, victim of her own epiphany.
I reached for a cigarette and had an epiphany of my own:
this sure beat the torpor of my habitual solitude.

In the capuccino bars, social workers keep the wolves at bay.
They say to their clients, 'Absolutely! You're not alone.
And anyway, the computers decide –'
I keep falling through history's elevator-shafts
into basements of mouldy, long-forgotten works,
which isn't the same as living and learning
who slaughtered whom at Actium
or did the gods really desert Antony
and so, keep all those undeserving lecturers on their toes.
Propertius applauded Caesar's returning legions,
cynically nodding off to their vulgar triumphs
while his lover's lap supported his heavy head
and his hands sweated with different hungers –
Propertius made less real by each whiff of direct experience.

I lay my head in the lap of the world.
I smell the musky damp of her sex.
It gathers on the inside of her thighs,
drops of corrupted rain that rub

against the folds of thickly petalled flowers
or like barrelfuls of venture capitalism's essence.
And though it is a warm day –
the air muggy, the sunlight heavy –
she's not aroused by my head's placement.
She's left cold by what I think and do.
And yet, I keep hoping for signs
that she's getting hot and bothered.
In this way, Propertius' lover, with glittering eyes,
searched for new prospects among the battle-weary,
looking to replace the poet's caresses –
his mild sense of justice, his native elegance –
with those of a one-armed soldier or a mystically inclined
astronaut. Who can blame her for saying, 'Propertius,
be a dear and go away. I'm tired of the truth.'

And so I learn Propertius was a Roman,
that wishing to be both child-like and corrupt,
he wrote poems to the love of his life
and didn't pretend that his citizenship fulfilled him.
He'd daydream his lover's attractions
and the four corners of the known world,
and she or the empire would appear to him
as a cloud of richly perfumed smoke.
So intangible still is the emotion of lust
that were it to find correspondence in an image
of poetry or black celestial bodies
the world would expire from gorging on itself.
It's no big deal to cultivate a little solitude
or to suck up the unanswered pain of brotherhood,
and, like most men, I befriend a favourite restaurant
and love the smell of roses and softball diamonds in the parks.

According to Kierkegaard, 1855

From an early age I pondered on Abraham.
How could an old man be so filled with dread?
He is always climbing a hill,
always searching a dark sky for signs –
a longing we satisfy with weakness and lies.
Abraham keeps muttering, 'Maybe it will rain.'
Lagging behind, Isaac keeps asking,
'Did you say something, Father?'
But Abraham admonishes the boy to be quiet,
or better still, to be invisible.

Frail in my body, at the end of thought,
it will be all over for me soon.
And now I'm inclined to recall other moments –
the hours Father and I spent reading,
warm by the fireplace in his book-lined room.
Putting aside a book, rising from his chair,
using a pet-name he liked, he'd say,
'Dreamer, let's grab our coats and stroll a little.'
Shouting for joy, laying down my fairy-tales,
I'd marvel that he knew my identity.
Throwing his head back, Father laughed.

How easy it is now to dismiss the memory
as mere pathos, as collusion with mere self –
the boy too small to reach the coats,
the father lifting him up so as to help.
In fairy-tales one pays for one's mistakes
with banishment to cold places or with death.
It is why I once believed Christ wept
if to do no more than honour obscure principles,
donating his twisted body to our imaginations.

And it is why poor Father now that we –
wrapped against winter, at large in the world –
teased me so much. 'Dreamer, we're lost,' he'd say –
I, of course, laughing at his silliness.
He meant only that, bound for the market,
we turned too many times on a familiar route,
about to visit the not-always-nice police instead.
And there was that time we turned up an alley
just as a man dropped to the ground
a hard, shiny object, then hurried off.
'A knife!' I cried, but Father disagreed.
In its place we found a few wilted flowers.

Throughout my career I balanced a love of Father
against this life-long hatred of Abraham,
pitting the melancholy of one against
the gloom of the other. Weak and religious, I knew
I'd have to wait and see if Isaac
could weather the passion that will always attract
the world's pathologies to a boy's body.
To what advantage could Abraham begin to know
everything large and small on his way
to a place of trial under a sky of dread?
And how often did he raise above the boy
the knife that demanded its due –
Abraham committed, his arm steady?

Eventually, hungry and thirsty, Father and I
would arrive at the market and mingle.
Bowing to everyone rich and poor,
Father traded news. Whether it was good or bad,
he spoke kind words, said nothing wrong,
and I admired him – more than I needed to –
for his tact and proud deference.
He'd give his orders to the merchants,
and from Father I acquired a taste
for drink – without which imaginary realms,
like that of the world, would be dreary.
But for the mind there are no shelters.

And if I have lived only to declare that,
then even now, old and useless as I am,
I dream how, naked, I stand before Father,
dumbfounded by this perpetual humiliation.

I grew older, hired expensive carriages,
and bringing with me costly wines,
I'd drive to the seacoast to drink and to brave
the storms. Sometimes, I fell into trances.
Sometimes, I slapped myself for no reason at all,
drunk from drinking more than libations.
Sometimes, it did seem my hands were agents
that worked more than one side of an argument,
that imagination is but the other cheek
we, so dire and holy, offer ourselves.
Remembering there our old childishness,
the zeal by which Father and I took hold
of a promenade or a romp through paradise,
I admitted that we had changed nothing.
It didn't matter if Father poked fun at fools
or turned to wink at comely widows,
saying he knew them to be merry souls!
Weary pilgrims in the end, we never left that study
of his, dreaming up those walks of ours.

How the boy loved his father for the play!
How sad it was to vacate the streets,
to abandon the victims of our innocent sport,
to remove our coats and hang them on the pegs –
Father promising there would be a next time.
Like Abraham frozen upon God's parched earth,
Father considered the angel's presence uncanny
but of little use in supplying relief from dread.
Even before I began to grow wise and drink,
there were the actual streets of Copenhagen
for which I turned out dressed in black, baiting
the passing ladies and gentlemen – I, the world's
wittiest scarecrow. And by wisdom I was endured.

And while there is still strength left to me,
let me put this matter straight:
It is only by some mental caprice
or by the light entering or leaving the room
that I've established love's lazy parameters,
the rightness or wrongness of my labours –
picturing how Abraham spent his emptiness,
the boy jumping up and down around him,
the ram spewing great jets of blood.
In the way dreams will follow one another
to flesh out the same crimes, the same nights,
I stand again – thin and stoop-shouldered,
crushed and naked – never far from my father,
soon to die in his eternal imagination.
Not once did he doubt the city he rebuilt
or that his life spelled death for someone.

I, Søren Kierkegaard,
who was always unwhole in body and mind,
with the usual cramp in my writing hand,
confess to having led a sedentary life.
To wit: that I laughed to no purpose
but to divest the pompous of their egos.
That I laughed at the poets for their fantasies,
at well brought-up ladies for their dreams.
That the laughter of angels was my puny defence
against Imagination's own offspring, Dread.
I renounced the world but did not negate it.
I drank and believed too much in fairy-tales.
I discussed existence with the Chief of Police
who wasn't a bad sort as policemen go.
I threw over a woman for the sake of my solitude,
leaving her to suffer the farce of marriage
to another – to tell lies and mop the floor.

Presumptuous in mind, I quarrelled with the Church,
whose officers understand nothing,
and I, knowing less, at least understood
Christ could not have wept for them –

there are no real tears in fairy-tales.
Roses give way to autumn leaves –
soon fog will blanket the city,
and I will have lived my life in precarious prayer,
unable to shout *love* like a child shouts *me*.
And as some ghostly victim of regret
begins to replace the avenging stones of the city
with weightier arguments – with heaven's vengeance –
what I've left to say isn't fit for anyone's ears.

At Cassiciacum

It is ancient earth, so the poets insist, and he –
his love of it not yet diminished,
come to these hills for a foretaste of judgment –
will carry it on his shoulders into paradise.
But as the sky lightens above the pines –
as though to see how tightly the chains are fastened –
he looks into their shadows, doubting his release.
Recalling the girl who had tormented his sleep,
she who had cradled in her lap the skull of the logos, he shudders.
It was always wet with the tears of women.
It was always encrusted with the salt of the oceans,
and she would offer him a taste of the beautiful rage,
and he would say 'yes' a little to her whims.

This skinny and unwell girl of the marketplace
laughed and idly remarked in those dreams,
'Augustine, but yours is a perilous vision of God.'
Like one craving death by drowning she floats in him –
she had shaken him to the depths of his being.
But to quiet and clear thoughts he and his mother came,
to a dawn streaked with rose-red hues –
ones a little more tired than those of the Creation.
And he can't help but notice how, already,
darkness reaches up for them – darkness of the pines,
of the old, blind poets, of pretence and vision.

To quiet they came, to happiness that has no substance
but whose splendour is Christ on his cross.
And, still fighting down this urge to say,
'At last I've been given something to know,'
he bends to his mother and receives a tempering kiss instead.
He came to see if a revelation will last.
He came to undo how it is that men possess truth.
And these are the four shouts of the mind
that require of everyone many tears:
Desire, joy, sorrow, fear – so many reasons to die.

Now he jokes to his mother, 'Mother,
I'm no longer a boy who gets teary-eyed for Dido!'

The wind picks up. The old olive tree creaks,
its silvery leaves lit with the sky's glow.
A few birds wheel above the hills,
and more take flight and climb
toward a smattering of clouds that are rose-edged.
Weeping in a garden in Milan he had cursed,
then surrendered his confusions to the Trinity,
unsure if he, himself, had broken down or come together.
'Mother, look how the face of God has frozen us here.'
Startled, and aged more than ever, she stares at her child.

To quiet they came, to something more than ideas.
To something not the sun, the burnished leaves, a few birds.
But to him the old urges return,
and if a man could talk, say, to a tree
and ask it – with some trepidation – 'Are you God?'
the tree would answer, 'No, but He made me,'
never dreaming in its purity that such a reply
could drive men to madness, to grief, at least –
to shout amidst the darkness of things.
Again there is the nightmare image of the girl
who had spoken to him but was not of himself.
From that dream he woke, saying, 'I and Thou, O Lord,'
and there came a way of living in the world.

Talk – it is another bridle for the throat.
Speech – it is another vanity. Terror – that is his reward,
and it is terror uprooting him again,
his mother bringing it on, saying this strange thing,
'Imagine the voice of God without the aid of the wind.'
They had talked throughout the night of love.
They had stood outside the house to know love.
Like a girl she kneels and picks violets,
pressing them to her ageing cheeks.
'Imagine that these flowers are only flowers,
that the rest of it – the grass and the stones…'

Remote now, unbelieving, she empties her hands
of what permitted her rashness.
'But you are right, Mother,' Augustine quickly answers.

To these hills they came neither penitent nor victorious,
and he has much to think on –
that to live in error is to harbour sickness,
that nothing will avert his mother's death,
that Adam was not separate until Adam knew speech,
that carried along by the cadences of thought
and life's circumstances, given to unalterable courses
of action, one is alone and one has solved nothing.
This exile is not what he wishes to endure –
the body of happiness that has no substance.
The space yawns wide again in his mind
where the dream-girl once displayed her attractions:
how it is that Time works, how it is that men desire.

This Business of June

Now she, too, has seen, has heard
what the month of June came to warn us about.
The flowers also – or did she notice? –
putting on gorgeous colours, curtsying,
bloomed and rippled in the breezes,
gave conscience to a standard charity:
how death often catches one short of scruples.
Even as one flips through newspapers,
says, 'Is it that easy to know a thing?'
or goes downtown on a sullen prayer
to shop for beach-towels at Woodwards,
one remembers that the season
benefits those who've made an art
out of reaching conclusions hassle-free.

Loneliness, the price of perms –
here in Vancouver or there in Budapest –
they are the paradises whose dues
Violet thought she might evade.
Yesterday, hers was the sugary life,
her wonderful figure the attraction
for the diners in the Old Europa.
'How unaffected the waitress is,' they said,
'so oblivious to her obvious charms –
though, truth to tell, she's moody.'
(Now she sits, moping at the counter.)
Not I, bursting with great themes,
but Dilemma itself confuses her,
how certain angels who, through pity,
were put to rest long ago,
have thrust their revamped programs
into appetites as coarse as our own.

Yes, June began with flowers
whose courtly manners were exemplary,
who, complimenting everyone on so little,

politely alluded to a painful past –
as when Malraux paid Mao a call.
(It's exactly what I mean to speak of:
history misrepresented, the melancholy –
a dominion Violet helps to establish
in a restaurant gone gloomy now.)
Visiting her homeland once, she found
a man who would take her in stride,
and he, fond of uproarious parties,
of Chuck Berry and gypsy music,
flies back to Budapest this weekend
to breathe his last at his mother's –
despite the food he's wolfing down.
Eventually, or much too soon, he will be finished
with life, with Violet – with the free and easy.
And if flowers do not misrepresent their purposes,
history and poems conspire to bore
this waitress – her rage worsening by the hour.

In between sniffles she talks
about what circulates in the restaurant,
but there's an extra serving of meaning
in those resentful eyes of hers –
as she brings the specials to the customers.
Who wants to be beaten at life's game
by both death and mother-in-law?
Then, to be left to this horrid patter,
dressed, as it is, in summer casuals,
of wages, China, vacations in Reno –
it's too thin and beside the point.
How undeserving we are of the words
we throw back at her hostile glare!

Often, flowers must steady in this light,
that they have complex vows to honour,
that theirs is no simple philosophy,
as when men, snapping fingers,
obtain sausages, beer and a flirtation.
Often, unexpected pain is best described

as a dream beginning to single one out.
'Damn these flowers!' I'll say when drunk,
referring to partly civilized things
whose perfume exists to mislead necessity,
to waft us toward barren moons.
I suppose we'll have violence by them as well,
if we must have tumours too,
that thrive, ghost-like, in exorbitant houses,
whose duration and effects
no two doctors can ever agree on.

There is kinship with numbers,
with what signifies or has volume,
as when astronomers pinpoint the darkest stars,
as when Violet broods, and I toast
this business of June: the departures.
It's because we'd rather not genuflect
to culture, science and politics
and so, barely notice their echoes
dying away on the paid-for TV.
And because my father died this June
in some out-of-the-way room,
I am prepared to accept Violet's digressions.
Should Karl die here, perceiving the mess:
right thoughts in Vancouver, tanks in Beijing?
Should he get cowardly, bank on what's sure:
Mother – who keeps an old house in Budapest?
These are dated questions. He's decided,
and he anticipates a slightly altered treatment,
granted his parole, his leave
from this city on a favoured coast.
Violet just said, 'As if it weren't enough,
he owed seven months on his Firebird.'

A dream struck the woman,
compelled her to put something in her voice:
a stunned self asking, 'What do I know?'
Sitting at the counter with calculator,
totalling a marriage's debts,

it is as if, by shouldering them,
feeding statements to the monster,
she might distract it into letting her off.
I'd been softened somewhat for the task
to hold a candle to her hardness,
and whether or not I misrepresent my work,
going on about flowers (they're just pretty now),
dwelling on the wrong extraneous intrusions,
the blooming and the curtsies keep coming,
insatiable, and only sometimes provident.

To Euripides

Our rooms await us again – in our friend's wild country,
So now, as in autumns past, having spent the year alone,
you'll gather the fruits of your study,
and trundle down the path from your island cave,
go to Athens, and book a fast ship – to join us in talk…
where we, the candles stinking, our friend's despotic eyes
glazed from wine and bad conscience,
will thrash out the evils of the day.
But this time, consider a long vacation.
The news from Athens isn't the best – so I hear,
and there are prospects more dreary
than drunken intellectuals and their games,
the endless verses, the garlands tossed at you
by men like me – in so many ways your junior.
What's to gain by returning to rogues,
men cowed by success and disaster?
Are you so keen on following the story?
Do you still plan to cop the first-prize – at your age?
And even if they don't haul you into court,
what of the body on its slow rack –
you a soldier who campaigned for four decades?
Besides, you say your tongue's gone listless,
and you can only think right and do wrong.
You remember your past affections as ailments –
the old friends in their foolish postures.
Compassion comes hardest when it's too late –
the players exhausted, broken down –
when hatred's spent and a regard for what happened
has run its course even in frauds like me.
Go back to Athens, impervious. But they will kill you.
Myself, I have my excuse handy: middle-aged shame.
Inform the company, should you visit,
that my old failure in battle – I knew it was all lost –
comes to haunt me with unusual vehemence.
Need I spell out again the time and the place,
and the numbers of men and ships I squandered,

51

that Poseidon took in without ceremony?
It's too tempting a topic: to let Thucydides off the hook,
when he might better choke on his lapses in solitude –
in this rude hut on this unforgiving coast.

An Exile of Excess

How to emulate instinct, dexterity,
to philosophize without causing ripples,
to best ignore that crystal sky
against which a violin's outburst
breaks into unattainable fragments...
the birds show us how it's done,
swallows swooping down one by one,
skimming across the pool for nourishment.
They put on a clinic, so to speak.
Worn deck-chairs, pots of flowers,
arbours, trellises, and even a buddha,
and figurines stuck in the shrubbery,
the apparatus heating the pool...
all these appurtenances one takes for granted
when tipsy or enthused enough:
that it resembles a movie-set,
or Pompeii in its more innocent days –
city planning in a socialist outpost.
'What we can't put into a machine,
we will lose – or something like that.'
So my host quotes from Carlyle,
formidable in his store of knowledge.

'Not drinking?' I ask, drunk myself.
'The glass is ceremonial,' he answers,
'all the inebriation I need.'
They couldn't have known, that snowy night,
when he and his wife reached the border
(the guards shot into the air),
that they'd wind up arguing so hard
with their freedom, with their neighbours.
Filling my glass again, he postulates
building-codes – drill compressors prohibited.
And, biting her lip, my hostess
(it's been 30 years, and only now

does she express her anger),
ventures to say that politics is irrelevant.

A moon shines through the rising heat.
A neighbour's garden belches fragrances.
And there's that cloying cedar-smell
so dear to the natives as they return
from respites spent among the real,
and the boughs of those cedars,
long used to an informal wilderness,
genuflect to this modest urban retreat.
Pope compared our souls to bottles:
a narrow neck makes pouring louder,
and I was gushing along smoothly.
'One fights, leaves, arrives somewhere –
maybe life gets better. But why should it?
It is, you see, how life is wasteful.'
My hostess just spoke of exile's principles!
Striking his glass so that it pings,
my host, not to be outdone, responds,
'Forces impinging on our bodies increase.'

I couldn't just sit and drink their wine –
surely the guest must contribute too.
But that was it for that evening –
the invitation has not been renewed:
to strip down, dive, get all wet,
smothering high culture's bubbles,
the detonations rising toward that moon.
'Oh, what fun!' my hostess grinned,
though my host would rather I had
bubbled with a quotation from Henry James –
on immortality. 'He's like that, you know,'
she said, describing her husband.

Politics might have defrayed the chaos.
Or would it be the same old pleasure
that those, so sanctioned, always take
in seeing their freedom inhabit daylight?

Not much left to tell of this tale:
I drove back through the quiet streets,
fought off local flora and fauna
that would have had me wrapped around lampposts.
'I've been out-romanced in life,' thought I,
passing the ex-mayor's modest bunker,
flipping it the usual votive salute.
But with that finger I stitch back together –
even now – the violin's scattered music....

Cultural Argument

You claimed unusual familiarity with death
(you're not poor Rilke, who said, 'Alles weg'),
but if you were here, *wurst* fouling your breath,
you'd praise these beggars who really beg.
Munich – a showplace. G.I.s gone Bavarian.
These dirty movies near my mountain birth.
Plaster Venuses, and maybe Herbert von Karajan
get the most out of the Songs of the Earth.
Bookseller, far off, black in your rage,
determined to undo the Canadian error,
from here I'd help you go on the rampage,
but this beer has no head for terror.
Such is the debate – in literature or elsewhere –
one's prowess both criminal and a matter of lies.

Abraham's Bemusement

Spotting their approach in the distance –
something of theirs glinting in the sun,
Abraham resumed his old position:
in the shade of the oak he slept.
When they arrived he had been dreaming.
Alarmed, Sarah cuffed him awake.
'There are strangers to greet,' she hissed.

Nor was he in the mood for company,
to play the role of the princely host.
To open his eyes and keep them open –
how like a hypocrite, like any liar.
The dream had severely shaken him:
how, all by himself, he'd become the world.
Inside him, the cities exploded.
The victims, with what innocence they could muster,
succumbing to fire, fled the inferno of his mouth.

Soon enough, the courtesies observed,
Abraham's meat and drink consumed,
Abraham resolutely faced the strangers.
Darkness blew stars across the sky.
He, determined to hold his own,
directed the talk to serious matters,
and the strangers shrugged as if familiar
with such rustic customs.
Earlier, Sarah had put it to them:
'You princes from a far-off place,
the old man you see is like old bread:
he's stale – the heat gone out of him.'

'The weariness of living,' Abraham answered,
setting jugs and cups in motion,
'and she has her own way with it.'
Still, as the evening wore on,
as Sarah grew younger and lovelier,

the years dropping from her face
like the leaves that fall to the earth,
Abraham craved an explanation
even as he ached from the development –
his flesh a rag, his mind a dry well,
the sky starlit but unsentimental.
Then Sarah began to hum in earnest
the songs she had sung at her wedding.
(And the strangers clapped their hands –
their wrists musical with bracelets.)

Abraham pressed harder for his respect.
So that he said, 'Once a man like me,
one who'd seen his fill of woe,
was called on to bargain with the gods
to spare the lives of the good
in cities slated for destruction.
The more he pleaded with the highest powers,
the more he began to believe –
regardless of their implacable will –
that he was the world's author.'

One of the strangers standing,
looking very much like an angel,
answered that Abraham was too proud.
'Every creature who inhabits the earth
would agree you took on too much,' he said.
Shamed and blushing, Abraham remembered
his wedding from a distant past,
in the streets of a great city:
wine, music and credit overflowing,
rabble and relations claiming portions,
men and women vaguely formed,
men and women complicating endeavour.

'I ask you,' Abraham kept on saying,
'just how much goodness in a city
will placate the forces of judgment?
One man? Twenty men? Fifty?

Better that there were none at all
to bring the matter up in the first place!'
The smiling strangers now on their feet
each answered with a different measure –
with voices growing increasingly perverse
at the futility of such questions.
And at last Abraham understood:
it's difficult to name a quantity,
and it's heartless to insist.
How abruptly the strangers departed
without saying where they'd come from –
bracelets softly jangling, amulets glowing,
eyes set in the same direction,
east beyond the sun-baked hills.

Now the sky turns opaque.
Smoke partially obscures the brightening.
The stars that had seemed so close before
fade and isolate the earth.
Wrapped in old skins, his head feverish,
leaning against the oak –
this marker of how far he's come –
Abraham attempts to speak the name
of any being not himself.
There had been much eating and drinking.
Then, the strangers gone off, he'd joined
with a creature smelling of a spring meadow.
(But it was that toothless old woman
whose brittle hair joins her smile to the ground.)

He says, 'Sorrow increased my pleasure.'
In this way, staring at her sunken cheek,
at the question of her true age,
he shivers and waits out the dawn.
And smoke drifts over the hills…
and Abraham draws his knees up tighter –
his wondering unusually burdened.

The Quarry at Syracuse

Sailing back to Athens, a survivor of the Sicilian Expedition tells the story of his internment and release.

Piraeus by dawn. Who'll be there
to greet us – if anyone, my friend?
And what stories will I tell?
This one? How that morning, come to gloat,
women peered down into our pit,
poured their perfume on our heads
so as to smother the stench of us?
Or is this what I have to relate –
of that hell-hole where we baked
and froze, such extremes of heat and cold
doing much to alter our features?
How handsome we became! They thought so,
sea-breezes parting their garments
so that their charms could also say
a thing or two about our condition.
So too, the hours of the sun and moon
are tailor-made, one might point out,
for men who grab spears, kiss ease goodbye,
leave to stewards and wives instructions
as to crops, livestock, rents, all else . . .
to come to this: diet rich in consequence:
putrid water, barley-dust and yes, other
distillations. The lucky forgot their farms,
the fare, seasoned with comedy, they had.

But the others died too slow
or couldn't stop up their ears in time –
the women showering our barracks with violets,
the women twittering down at us,
'Spread your wings and fly up, you men,
and let's dance away the morning!'
So, when we, attired in our wounds,
married to rock, did reach up
for the vision, they were clearly amused.

And then...to consider singing!
My god, what presumption on our part!
Well, it's not so easy as that
to show the stuff one is made of –
the moisture squeezed out of you,
wounds hissing with humiliation and pus.
Some say there's a second nature
that runs more deeply than any first
(or merely skips on ahead of calamity),
but let me just say: we sang.
The mouth opened. The throat strained
to dredge up what had gone so far underground
(a purge might've been useful then) –
the tongue sitting there like a dead bird.
Yet, something in me and my comrades
(my hatred more lively) smelled freedom,
began to consider the vertical life again
and bring Euripides to the provinces...
because, out of nothing, it began with song,
song of a moonless night, of worthless strategies,
of incompetence favouring Athenians less.
What more is there to tell an old poet
to whom I sail with our thanks?
I could relent, just remind him of this:
'Poetry that comes between us and horror –
what a sweet thing it is, a godsend!
So human, yet so divorced from our kind.'
On the other hand, say we brought the house down
and delivered ourselves from Syracuse.

Toward the Angel of the Flaming Sword

To ask 'Where to from here?'
to uphold the myth that our hearts are broken,
will barely pay us adequate or redeeming wages.
But sometimes as we kiss, as the angel stands
(deep in your eyes) on guard,
the earth around that fearsome presence
heated to glass, the beating of our hearts
grows alien to us, charred like selves
that remain stubbornly luminous, beyond recognition.
So then our dull, prosaic minds must do,
and we must fall back on our ageing caution,
and once more gain this abrasive asbestos earth.
Still, we came into this existence to taste love.
Still, the angel in his suit of fire will not be dislodged.
And if we continue to kiss in the safety of where we hide,
we cannot help but advance our camouflage one step each time.

Shakespeare in Verona

You birds –, you toughs with claws and beaks,
broken like me by the light at birth,
you skitter over the stones and the ground,
and peck and screech. In this way, I inflate my work.
To high and low, I gave my fooling.
Even as, through injury, I spoke my piece,
it was theatre to those who came for poetry.
I exacted revenge with beautiful poisons,
and now this age inspects the pollutions.
Still, at the end of the corso Cavour,
in the tiny square just off the street,
so forlorn a nook with the yellow leaves
a gardener swept into lonely piles, I sit.
Here's the stunted palm, the bedraggled cypress.
The Arch of the Gavi is baleful stone,
a desolate tooth in its gum of earth –,
and I, come to rest in the argument,
meet you Montagues and Capulets.
You tear at the litter along with the bees,
and you cross one another with your ancient weapons.
Here it is: hunger, bite, sting – old songs.
Over there, a waiter spreads open his newspaper,
backhands the thing into submission,
scans the opinions and skips to the sports,
his shadow debating the daily orders:
his progression through the vanities…to some year 2000,
and his cigarette sets fire to the obituaries.
If, elsewhere, dreamless hands caress
the museums of the word and flesh – here, a man jumps,
brushes his pants clear of offending ash,
miffed as any daredevil who's ruined a shirt.
Then, those Africans there –, they turn aside and snicker.
Uprooted, they drain their cans of Coke,
and a schoolgirl taunts her boy into testing his mettle.
Just so, Dante saw the lovers doing it,
then compressed into the kiss a downward spiral –,

and he buried the results in hell.
I shrug – like any ghostly instance of perjury would,
and between the palisades of shining teeth,
the girl sticks out her tongue,
and together, the lovers, lap to lap,
rub haunch to thigh, and grind the lazy hour into a jewel....
Pain pursues pleasure –, the chase inspiring music.
Save for critics, everyone sees through the trick.
The memory of a select few, if generous to all,
was too big an ardour to trust – to a mere critique.
So, I have been to the cathedrals to escape
the heat of committed minds, and I have said, 'Not yet',
and have stepped over the drifters on the stairs,
and have joined with the crowds in the streets,
and, with them, exchanged love's thin veneers.

They come just now to sit and converse.
They are assured like art once was –
the signora and the signora.
And they tuck their bottoms to a seat,
and, white-haired, lipsticked, powdered, they say,
'It's true', and, 'Oh, how sad –',
investing so many acts with more rights and wrongs
than any actor, on his form, cares to remember.
The bells toll and the horns blare,
and with his worn stump of a cane,
the old sun taps against the newer goods....
Well, I tell you, you birds who hog your crumbs,
he who wrote John and gave Christ His soul –
when he thought: 'Sweet World of Worlds'
he meant: 'Even the Light has its Clamour'.
And the women knit, and with their eyes
they polish the molar – that Roman thing –
that announced a triumph long agonies before
the apostles blasted their entry into the void.
Put away this farce? No, it prospers –:
this town is so nearly lovely on its plain.
Birds mock birds, women snip flowers,
and lovers, by their kisses, wipe

64

egregious relevance from the word.
As for me, back through the arthritic autumn,
there's the pensione whose starved concierge
sucks the hearts from her chocolates,
irons the bedsheets, blinks at the TV.
A room, I suppose, with a crucifix
and a bulb of pitiful wattage...
And the review, of course.
I can imagine its suppressed fury –:
'Shakespeare, whom we brothers and sisters
expunge from the brotherhood and sisterhood of text,
performed, this day, as though on a whim.
It remains unclear if he will ever recover
his mandate, his immoderate achievement –,
but it is assumed that, if we relent,
and life returns to his gaudy complaints,
and he poisons us again with character,
he will liken his chamber of operations –
his skull – to a sleep of rouged walls,
and blush like a virgin for the sky
when it swings by to propagate the seasons
with the good, and with the evils that will finish the job.'
So you have it, you toughs with claws and beaks.

Thanksgiving

He is still at it, counting the rooms.
Every night he goes the rounds
as if he could increase the credit
of a surfeit of space
and find in that his power.
To tryst, to pray, to hide away?
It is all this and more:
the sublime painter whom all admire
just wanted to rent a palace!
I have tried to count the rooms myself
and left off with the gardens,
although my father said to me
that there is in space
a kind of pleasure –
a dilemma that will outlast the house.
Now he has come to dine with us –
he who has remembered us,
but dinner will need some warming up.

The flesh itself – it is no burden,
so his mentor had taught him,
to use light and dark, to live,
grandly, off the proceeds.
Now for his mistress – a kiss.
An affectionate pat for the son
who's so untalented
but is rather precocious.
And, bad day or not, I will catch
my mentor short of a response....
Yes, hear me out: I speak of Greeks
who, driven here by Turks,
gather in nearby churches
to grouse about and pray.
I deem such behaviour unreasonable:
no event, consolation arrives too late.

66

Indeed he would: my father wearily recalls,
'But that is what God is there for.'

How lovely her shoulders still are,
lustrous in warm candlelight,
discreet beneath her shawl of lace.
And I, courteous boy,
I sometimes seem to please –
as should the musician admitted to the room just now.
If my father has been unwell,
his renown, so wide, faded lately,
he could paint his way back to health,
physician and patient in one,
pallid face, pleading eyes in a single healing!
The game would show the future
how he alone has kept his head
against Torquemada's legacy
that some call truth and others torture.
Stretching limbs, attaching hands,
exquisite feet to his victims,
throwing them into a state of rapture,
my father has already reflected something of these days.

The lesser artist of the two
(compared to Michelangelo,
who always shut himself away),
my father, punctual with a contract,
misquoted that day in Rome long ago,
would have done the thing differently.
He would have lavished the ceiling of that chapel,
not with heavy souls, tons of flesh,
but with notions infinitely more tragic.

Fire, fluff comprise our condition,
nobility of mind and spirit no more
than rumours of miracles, traces of smoke....
What's left but to snuff the candles,
and to praise the meal again!
'Musician, strike a melody of thanksgiving.

We have sinned but, I think, in time,
some will appreciate our errors' –
so my father appeases opinion.
His mistress, rising, brushes at tears.
A lovely dinner, as it turned out,
so there's no need for malice
even if it is aimed at myself.
It is my cue. To the rescue!
'Mother, Father is tired.
He raises his face and shuts his eyes.
Like a bird bringing its wings together,
he folds his hands. I think he prays for us,
but he also plans to paint
a place devoid of any presence.'

At the palace of Villeña, Toledo, 1604

The Astrologer's Letter

Will I, my friend, with charts or not,
divine what I observed, today,
in Diocletian's vegetable-patch?
The wind came up suddenly,
and the man, once Caesar,
one of four to a quartered empire,
now shaking his fist, now smacking his head,
exclaimed, 'Of course, Byzantium!'
For once, I thought him misguided.
Well, I am in demand these days.
So many want the future known.
But woe to him who fails to match
the right prize to the right person!
As for Diocletian – he's gone rustic.
Twenty years of empire does it,
brings on the urge to forget
how doom behaves inside men.
Out with the tiara, the jewelled slippers,
with spies and brooding generals,
ambassadors and countless minions!
On with an old coarse garment
to raise cabbages, no less!
It's quite beyond my comprehension.
Doom I know, born into it.
There it was infecting the earth.
And Diocletian nursed this mother of us all
with broths of cold passion and gall,
in order to say, in the end, 'I retire.
Twenty years. Enough. Or else,
crazed soldiers will call the shots
and their sons sink the throne in blood.'
Indeed, three caesars and their armies
bent their wills to him that long.
And if one will go among cabbages,
it is better done barefoot –
one specimen in particular attracting him.

The thing is huge, and perhaps it does
resemble Constantine's rude head
(but I think it's much prettier).
Still, there is emptiness at its core,
superstition and resilience –
gods, demons and the occasional mortal
deriving equilibrium from the mixture.
Byzantium though? What can it mean?
And what does it portend for us
that the man would put a question
to a vegetable, to some splendid green rose, if you will,
and, patting that monster, suddenly cringe from it?
Policy... it's but a charm born partly
of ephemerality and reason,
and if he's done with weaning from shabbiness
consistent rule and regular borders,
Constantine has cunning enough
to tear the world apart
just to make it whole again.
It's beyond me, you see, but then,
ours is the weakest of arts,
and for want of decent numbers
the stars grow parched in their constellations.
Which is to say, there's trouble ahead,
and, if we were to know the future,
we'd shorten what future remains to us.
Only this: just as earlier, when he, in a rush,
ploughed into me in the courtyard,
spun around and went out the gates
to his favourite plot of earth,
so he came away from his prizes,
getting drunk on rain – the storm in full force,
and it was clear that he was shaken.
Farewell. And may ignorance keep us safe!

Constantine went on to eliminate his rivals and unify the empire, only to divide it among his sons, who, in turn, finished one another off: the vicissitudes of hereditary succession. If Diocletian died before he could get to him, he managed to have the old emperor's wife and daughter beheaded. His real achievement, according to Burckhardt, was to recognize that, among the religions, only Christianity had any real vigour. Accordingly, he aligned himself with it, and on this basis erected his state.

Claudius

Instead of keeping quiet about his stupidity,
Claudius explained, in a number of speeches, that
it had been a mere mask assumed for the benefit of
Caius, and that he owed both life and throne to it.
Nobody, however, believed him.

It's an age, really, for humourists,
for those less vulgar to shut their mouths –
so my women and slaves proscribe whole lists,
but I sin a little less than a mouse.
If there remains in the world a mind
familiar with the urge to reticence,
it won't want allusions at this time
to the intemperate terrors of this palace.
The more I keep scribbling away
the more it's virtually guaranteed
Time will overlook what I had to say –
the wife stilling me and my organ of seed.
Yes, Mother said I was no dynast:
Nature begat me, then lost interest.

Good Friday

Tear up the letter you are writing,
simply reflect on the obvious:
here, a baby may even mediate
between tangibles and intangibles,
where, in the hotel lobby,
the TV tuned to a biblical flick
offers dark-suited men opportunities
to guffaw at Victor Mature's antics.

Here, it should be plain by now:
the body of redemption is large,
as large as the town has rooms available,
no one of them to remain vacant
and – despite the German couple in argument –
the scene of serious discourse.
Boys went about in black robes today,
and thorny crowns fell over their eyes,

and, between mouthfuls of sweets, they joked,
climbing Agrigento's steep hills.
Whereas now, weekend revellers drink,
and, banging on the doors of WCs,
wine-gassed, crooning 'Open sesame,'
they yell that they can't hold it.
It's a pure science: self-adoration –
attendant shadows gossip of some agony,

toothbrushes and travel brochures
agitating toward a sky of cold stars.
It has its own brass band: this emptiness,
and the bells, producing their effect –
atonement that has passed from literature –
have set your teeth on edge:
that when wine and religion begin to matter
it would seem that nothing else does.

The Praetorian Guard

A week into summer, the weather hot,
beneath a large and luminous moon,
she kneels and puts flowers in their pots,
coaxing the earth to adhere to roots –
to treat the new cuttings well.

Then, going to wake him, she says, 'Come look!'
and speaks the word *progeny*.
She means to say *sedition* –
her eyes going on to explain:
'We have to ponder something.'
Rubbing his eyes, he answers, 'Yes,'
and adds, as some ambulance wails,
'No doubt your instincts are secure.'

Behind schedule – it is midnight,
triangulating flower, moon and wife,
he says, 'These old flowers remind me of old paintings.'
There is fickle space, uncommitted time,
and these spaces and times that they,
as newlyweds, have indulged –
until one begins to perceive the paradox:
the Great Doings always lie beyond
one's going back to the infinite,
and a helpful sky does creep closer
as she sets petunias in a row.
(Swirling about in its lustrous robes,
it penetrates her senses,
steals state secrets from the nervous blooms.)

How the hours of revelation
seep into his own hyper-emptiness –
what with the heir to the ages: America
bugling away just over the border...
so that he may as well perish,
in a Vermeer's pearly glow, from dubious attitudes.

73

How his hand began to grope
for a spot unspoiled and cool,
or, at least, for traction on the pillow –
when she roused him and said, 'It's time.'

*

Through the bedroom door she dragged him –
into vastness, into theology
reeking of Domestica and oblivion,
of jumbo jets perforating the sky.
'That flower,' he says, regarding one,
'purple, it illuminates death,
and the moon, in turn, illumines the flower,
revealing the stencilling on the petals:
Et in Arcadia Ego.
Death is also there
where proportion leads to bliss.
You see, I remember – sort of.'
'I'm so tickled,' she answered, 'that you do.'

And it's a great deal of slogging too,
to humbly light the candles of passion
so as to find the best ways and times
to arrive at places where she'd be touched.
But with arms steeped to the elbows in dirt,
she has stooped so low as to deny events,
and, what's more, she has repudiated their primacy.
She has helped him, but it has been difficult.

She pulls him back inside with a jerk.
'Husband,' she jokes, disrobing herself,
'bitterness overflows, despite your care.
Draw some of it off for me.'
'Is there a place without it,' he asks,
'where flowers, though shy, stabilize
the rising and falling of our breathing,
and the velvety elements in which we swim?

Never has your voice so mocked the means
by which we consume one another's usual tact.'

'You must look at my flowers,' she whispered,
'how they perch like birds of rare plumage,
how they will go before us in exile
over deserts of law, through cities of godly song.'
So they linger with them (from a distance) –
with each red and blue and purple bloom.
And mouth meets mouth and limb clasps limb,
and the flowers, converging on their seclusion,
muffle the cries of their bravery, decency and doom.

The Eternity Club

In the restaurant, tired and wilted,
the diners tough out the heat.
Drawing relief from the suds they drink,
they butter bread and manage to eat.
Now the social-worker parks herself
among these men, sour and dour,
and in her pale-blue, stylish dress,
she sits with briefcase and allure.

There's religion in the cigarette smoke,
but what's in affection to esteem –
now that her smile inexorably grows
into a tense but mobile theme?
If a hero in the press sometimes,
she's just a worker in her own eyes,
tattooing the table with red nails,
waiting, waiting for her pyrogies.

Yes, when calculators bite into Time,
something two-stroked grinds in Dakar.
But when the data's at her fingers,
flash fleshes out our global bazaar.
Maybe I add to her stress somewhat,
relying too much on these maps I've got:
items I've dreamed, that the heat makes bright –
as with blazing trees subdividing light.

'There's less to darkness than we know,
and there's more to it than we show.'
So say these oracles, also saying, 'It's not workable' –
these heart-shaped pale imitations of the world.

It's evening now, the place soon to close,
diners leaving like they can't depose
the despair with which she, social-worker, pays
the disease she hadn't expected to avoid, these days:
all those fatally depressed –
she so fruitful in her blue dress.
But I stray too far from my topic:
how failure advances through sheer logic.

My Continuing Education

For Erling Christensen

Somehow, between us, it is fitting to say,
despite defeat, all else that comes,
that we will argue away the nights,
drink and resist one another's reconstitution.
Because it is your resource: probability,
you understand then life's inconvenience: dilemma.

And isn't this, too, a ticklish dilemma –
despite defeat, what's fitting to say:
reminders of our decline (tedious probability),
is to your house what often comes?
To smoke less may be your reconstitution,
but your friends . . . they're the state some nights.

They bring to your parties on certain nights
a kind of reformation. And this group-dilemma
who, in sneakers, in lipstick (their reconstitution),
will, with the *sangfroid* of authority, often say,
'From some lost affair of the Left I knew you!' It comes,
and I reply. 'Wrong again . . . in all probability.'

But on them the humour is lost . . . in all probability.
Bleary-eyed, pissed, one should disregard their nights,
or look around and eyeball what comes:
those who have risen from the ashes of dilemma.
They are the state when they modestly say
they are changing it – so heed your reconstitution!

I'll tell you how due is love's reconstitution –
right around the corner it is . . . in all probability.
Contravening law, poets make law and say,
'There's security in our union, in our bars at night
when we sit and examine the paradox
that what we write we write as circumspectly as it comes.'

Avoiding them, because along with them come
such perfect egos, virtue and reconstitution,
I come to you, sorely missing the old dilemma
of what was human, and in all probability,
more human. To you who request my presence some nights,
to drink wine, to argue, to embrace, I say:

Let us drink, argue and embrace dilemma,
give ourselves an A plus come what may
to slap the old C minus to our nights.

The Tree in Luigi's Moka Restaurant

While there is still time and a reason to,
let me tend the reputation of an old poet I know.
Before his name truly passes into oblivion,
before he starts to rant against everything and nothing,
boring good-natured nurses from a hospital bed,
I can think of no other act more fitting –
indeed, it's the only decent thing to do –
than to laud his prolific works.
To begin, there is no such person,
regardless of the thousands of authors
listed in compendiums, directories – in *Who's Who*.
But, just as my verses are a hoax,
my dim career a self-imposed fantasy,
I'll perpetrate the legend of an old martyr –
one who, if he could take it all back,
would still pump his poems up with spite,
who's sufficiently in funds this evening
that he can foot the bill for dinner
and pretend to suffer in significant measures of pain.

We walk into Luigi's as the sun is setting.
Mario the waiter takes our order.
And as the old poet watches him prance away,
he says, 'There's a married man who has mistresses.
I, too, have trucked so much with love
that save in the minds of keeners
I doubt if it exists any longer.' What's stranger
than to hear a man quote from his poetry?
Anyway, someone is playing the accordion,
and an old couple is dancing alone,
growing a little younger together, and more aged,
while friends and family pound the tables
with spoons, shouting out endearments.
Then the one-man band takes a break
and little girls storm the coveted jukebox.
There's hockey on the TV – the sound's off,

and Mario talks up a lonely divorcée.
'A nice place,' the old poet observes, his eyes
riveted to the lovely figure of a young woman
who crosses the dance-floor to join the girls.
'Life is, after all, a well-known secret,' I tell myself,
'that robs poets of their glory.' It is also bizarre
to silently quote one's own verse.

Thankfully, the old poet isn't moved enough
by the sight of people at their best
to recount tales of his love-affairs,
sparing me the sexual grotesqueries.
We eat, drink and smoke, and, this time,
I squelch an impulse to brag of my new poem –
though I'm proud of its complicated imagery.
He'd just wave his cigar about anyway,
suddenly finding it all a profound irritant,
muttering that these things take years.
But as the time passes he notices the tree,
and, suspicious, eyeing the thing
that stretches from the floor to the ceiling,
he asks, 'So what's it made from? Paper?
Love? Collective guilt? Bad dreams?'
I answer, 'Okay, it's a presumption,
but it reminds the people of their homeland.'
The old poet snorts, 'Sorry I bothered,'
and he seeks after another woman to ogle
while another poem of mine bites the dust.

How to tell him then that this tree
is my paean to dying, out-of-order worlds?
That here as lovers court each other
and families attempt to sit at table together
and lonely men watch the hockey game
and single women recross their legs,
this unremarkable imitation of nature,
in its garishness, cries its invisible tears.
That jewelled dragon-flies with ugly faces –
ones nearly as gross as the old poet's –

mate on the wing alongside its boughs,
that it wouldn't take much to imagine
how the dance-floor is a moon-swept lake,
how, as the cities burn, poets dream,
how Mussolini swings upside-down, disgusted –
as silent and ineffectual as all charms are –
how we all listen to the wind in the leaves
and some hear romance, sex, god or contempt,
and others are inspired to write verses
that go off in the mind like steel traps –
that the old poet aged too fast, jammed between
knowledge and death.

Oh, I think that had I caught the old poet
in a mood more agreeable to my fantasy,
I'd have chatted away, inventing our mutual demise,
sliding easily in and out of desperate lives –
like Baudelaire on a leisurely bender with God.
As it is, I would have outraged my friend.
As it is, he's made me call him a cab,
and there he sits, waiting, at peace with himself,
with the world and with his dark career.
Attired in a painfully bedraggled suit,
sporting a nose as red as a cherry bomb,
he talks of who is finished,
and remembers to add, 'Not that anyone cares.'
Occasionally, he'd gotten his hackles up,
venting his spleen against some crystalline nest –
one befouled with imagination, ideas,
to be wiped clean with zealotry and blood.
As it's wicked of me to keep up for so long
this charade of a hero, I'll get real. Here's the taxi.
The driver honks. I usher the old poet out,
saying, 'Be good, and I'll see you in the spring.'

I'll order another coffee and just sit for now.
I'll listen to Mario whistling in the dark –
he, lighting his liquid eyes with angels
while the goddesses of pain and patience share

their pearls and veils and gossip of boys.
He'll keep his absurd dignity intact –
as the world's broken bits fuse into an unreal dream
like lovers do when they kiss on TV,
conspiring to be both compassionate and cruel.
It is all growing to dimensions so vast
no ancient curse can hope to shatter it,
and no citizen will casually undercut the miracle
with another objection born of fear and a bread-line.
And I, though no longer enraptured,
will water the tree with praises,
leaving to others the game of oracle,
trusting that the old poet will enjoy his rest.
I'll say, 'To the tunes of Virgil, to old yankee
democrats, the earth does try to recall itself –
its rivers, mountains, wild dust.'
It appears, sometimes, even in these dubious hours,
that the world has come this far on far less.